P9-DBU-610

# Holiday Cookies

SUGAR COOKIES, PAGE 18

# Holiday Cookies

Juliette M. Rogers

Photographs by Michael Grand

CRESCENT BOOKS
NEW YORK • AVENEL, NEW JERSEY

**A FRIEDMAN GROUP BOOK**

This 1993 edition published by Crescent Books, distributed by Outlet Book Company, Inc., a Random House Company, 40 Engelhard Avenue, Avenel, New Jersey 07001.

Random House
New York • Toronto • London • Sydney • Auckland

ISBN 0-517-08773-1

*HOLIDAY COOKIES*
was prepared and produced by
Michael Friedman Publishing Group, Inc.
15 West 26th Street
New York, New York 10010

Editor: Dana Rosen
Designer: Stephanie Bart-Horvath
Photography Editor: Christopher C. Bain

Typeset by Bookworks Plus
Color separation by Excel Graphic Arts Ltd.
Printed and bound in Hong Kong by Leefung-Asco Printers Ltd.

8 7 6 5 4 3 2 1

*T*his book is dedicated to Cita, who finds a
reason to name any day a holiday, and
celebrates it with just the right cookies.

Zahra's Peanut Feqqas Cookies, 70

*R*ecipes, like cookies, are meant to be shared with friends. My sincere thanks to all
those cooks who have shared their favorites with me and my family, especially to
Dixie Gurian, Maria Sibley, and Kitty Morse.

# *T A B L E       O F*

*I*ntroduction   page 9
*B*asic Baking Guidelines   page 10
*P*acking and Shipping of Holiday Cookies   page 14
*T*he Recipes   page 16

Sugar  Cookies   page  18  ★  Decorator's  Frosting   page  19  ★  Royal
Icing   page  19  ★  Peppermint  Candy  Canes   page  20  ★  Christmas
Card  Cookies   page  21  ★  Stained  Glass  Windows   page  22  ★  Penn-
sylvania  Dutch  Almond  Cookies   page  24  ★  Modeled  Gingerbread
Cookies   page 26  ★  Gingerbread  Cookie  Place  Cards   page 27  ★  Pe-
can  Snowballs   page  28  ★  Spanish  Wind  Wreaths   page  29  ★  Spicy
Pfeffernuesse   page 30  ★  Kerstkransjes   page 31  ★  Moravian  White
Christmas  Cookies   page  32  ★  Cinnamon  Stars   page  34  ★  Lebku-
chen   page 35  ★  German  Fruity  Spritzes   page 36  ★  Pecan  Speculas

# CONTENTS

page 38 ★ German Chocolate Pretzels page 39 ★ Brandied Butter Wreaths page 40 ★ Caramel Dream Bars page 41 ★ Holiday Linzer Cookies page 42 ★ Orange Oatmeal Bars page 44 ★ Chocolate Bars page 45 ★ Southern Hospitality Lemon Bars page 46 ★ Orange Roll Cookies page 48 ★ Chocolate Almond Shortbread page 50 ★ Snowflake Spritzes page 51 ★ Chocolate Cherry Nut Squares page 52 ★ Portuguese Cocoa Cookies page 53 ★ Chewy Peanut Cookies page 54 ★ Greek Easter Cookies page 56 ★ Hazelnut Cookies page 57 ★ Passover Macaroons page 58 ★ Pumpkin Goblins page 60 ★ Cranberry Boggers page 61 ★ Old Maine Lace Cookies page 62 ★ Polar Bear Claws page 64 ★ Clipper Ship Hermits page 66 ★ Chocolate Orange Cheer Cookies page 68 ★ Zahra's Peanut Feqqas Cookies page 70 ★ Conversion Chart page 71
Index page 72

8

*Introduction*

It would be hard to imagine an occasion when cookies would not be welcome. After school with a glass of milk, late in the afternoon with a cup of carefully steeped tea, as a quick snack, or passed around the room with the coffee after dinner, cookies are as versatile as they are delicious. As a gift, they offer the chance to show that you care enough about someone to spend your time and talent creating something special for them. Whether delivered hot from the oven on a plate to your next-door neighbor or shipped halfway around the world, nothing says "home" quite like cookies.

*E*ach culture has its own special holiday cookies, with recipes that have been passed down from one generation to the next. Grandmother's cookies are often the first recipes young people ask for when they set up their own kitchens. This book is a collection of the traditional holiday cookie recipes of many cultures and families, for sharing cookie recipes is a timeless tradition all its own.

*Basic Baking Guidelines*

**B**efore you start your holiday baking, you should familiarize yourself with a few things. First of all, read and understand your recipe. Check for any unusual ingredients you may not have on hand, any special equipment that is required, or any advance preparation you should do, such as chopping nuts or sifting flour before measuring. Once you've done this, assemble your ingredients and tools. Grease your pans, if necessary. And, perhaps most important, leave time for your cooking—half the joy of holiday food comes from preparing it!

*T*here are many terms and procedures in cooking that you may not be familiar with. All of the terms you need to know for the recipes in this book are listed below.

*Transfer to Wire Racks:* There are racks for cooling baked goods, which are readily available in kitchen supply stores. The racks allow cookies to cool quickly because air circulates under them. Set out the racks on a flat, clean surface. To transfer cookies, use a pancake turner or metal spatula, lightly dipped in flour, and slide it underneath them. Place the cookies in a single layer on the racks.

*Cream:* Completely incorporate shortening and sugar. When recipe specifies to cream until light and fluffy, you should use an electric mixer if possible, and beat until sugar is no longer very grainy, and the texture is smooth.

*Separate Eggs:* To separate an egg, gently crack the shell on the edge of a bowl or counter. With both hands, pry the two halves apart over a bowl, carefully tipping the egg yolk into one of the halves and letting the whites fall into the bowl. Gently transfer the yolk to the other half, getting rid of as much white as possible. Be very careful not to break the yolk, because if any gets into the whites, they will not whip correctly.

*Beat Egg Whites:* Many recipes require that you beat egg whites into various stages. First is the foamy stage, where the whites will still be liquid with a frothy top layer. Further beating will produce soft peaks. You can tell this stage when you lift the beater from the whites, and a soft peak which droops over on top is left. Stiff egg whites will leave a perfect peak at this test. It's easiest to beat egg whites with an electric hand mixer, but it is possible to do by hand, so long as you have the will. Don't add sugar to whites before beating, or they will not whip correctly.

*Fold:* Incorporate ingredient(s) into a lighter mixture (usually egg whites) using a smooth, rolling stir. This is best done with a rubber spatula. Add the new ingredient(s) to the light ingredient(s). Starting at one side of the bowl, slowly stroke the spatula in a circular motion through the bottom mixture and wrap over the top mixture, using the narrow blade (not the broad side) of the spatula to lead. Bear in mind that the purpose of this is to prevent deflating the light, whipped mixture any more than necessary. Continue the slow stirring until both mixtures are combined.

*Sift:* Sieve dry ingredients to lighten, get rid of lumps, and mix together. If you do not have a sifter, you may substitute a fine wire strainer. Place dry ingredients in the strainer over a bowl. Lightly tap the sides of the strainer or stir gently with a spoon.

*Cut in Butter or Margarine:* Using a pastry blender or a fork, this means to cut butter up into small lumps within a flour mixture. This is not mixing, because you want butter or margarine pieces remaining, averaging ¼ inch in size.

*Toast Nuts:* Place nuts in a dry frying pan. Shake pan over a medium flame for a few minutes. As soon as you can smell the nuts, remove pan from the heat and slide the nuts onto a plate. Be very careful not to burn the nuts.

*Double Boiler:* Used for slow cooking and melting on the stove top, this set-up consists of a base pan full of water and a nesting top where the cooking is done. If you don't have one, you can easily make one, with a metal bowl on top of a saucepan of water slightly smaller than the diameter of the bowl. The bowl should sit partially in the pan, but never touch the water. Watch out for steam burns when cooking this way.

*Citrus Peel or Zest:* To obtain the peel of a citrus, you need a zester, which gives a ready-to-use peel. If you do not have a zester, you can use a vegetable peeler and a knife. Peel off the colored rind of the fruit you are preparing, and slice it into very narrow slivers, no bigger than ½ inch long by ⅛ inch wide.

*Floured Surface:* Whenever a recipe requires rolling out the dough, you should flour your work surface beforehand, unless the recipe specifies differently. This is to prevent the dough from sticking. You should flour your surface lightly, using a sifter or strainer, to barely cover it. The more flour you use, the tougher your cookies will be, so use it sparingly. Chilling dough makes it less sticky, so if you run into sticking problems, let your dough chill for ½ to 1 hour, until it is firm.

*Cookie Cutters:* You can find these in every shape imaginable, to fit any holiday. By far the most effective type is the metal-outline type, with an open top. If you don't have any cookie cutters, you can cut circles with the rim of a glass, or use a knife freehand to cut other simple shapes.

*Oven Temperature:* Oven thermostats are not always reliable. If you find that your cooking times seem to be off, you may want to get an in-oven thermometer to get an accurate reading of the real temperature and then adjust your oven's temperature setting accordingly. Also, you must preheat your oven to the required temperature before you put the cookies in. A good time to do this is when you start putting cookies on sheets, or when you start making a fast recipe, such as a bar cookie. You will learn to get a feel for how long it takes your oven to heat.

*Baking Sheets:* Most cookies are baked on these. There are many varieties, from heat insulated to no-stick, but which kind you use is up to you. Pay special attention to whether the recipe calls for a greased or ungreased baking sheet. If the recipe calls for a greased sheet, grease it in advance, regardless of what type of sheet you use.

*Packing and Shipping of Holiday Cookies*

Nothing could be more welcome to a far-off friend or family member than a surprise care package of holiday cheer. It's amazing how a tin of frosted hearts can brighten up someone's lonely Valentine's Day! You need only use a little extra effort to make your homemade goodies shipping-proof.

Choose to bake cookies that keep well. Those using honey and oatmeal are particularly suitable, as they maintain moisture. Avoid bars with a custard or creamy layer, or anything that is perishable, unless you can send them chilled.

14

Cookies that are thick, or soft and chewy, will ship better, while crisp cookies break more easily in the mail. If you choose to ship fragile cookies, pack them carefully.

When packing, make sure to completely separate moist and crispy cookies, in their own air-tight wrappings. You should also keep strongly flavored cookies apart, so the dominant flavor won't be adopted by the more delicate cookies.

All types of cookies or bars cannot be wrapped the same way. Small, decorative cookies can be put into individual paper bonbon or cupcake wrappers, which come in holiday patterns. Sticky bars should be wrapped in waxed paper to prevent them from sticking together.

Pack cookies into a sturdy cardboard box to ship. If you are shipping sugar cookies or another thin and breakable variety, the cookies should be packed in a protective container to prevent crushing. An attractive decorative tin used to guard the cookies can even serve as a double gift. Fill in any extra space in the cookie box or tin with loosely crumpled waxed paper or colored tissue. If you are sending many items within a large box, put smaller, individual boxes or tins on the bottom, substantial cookies on top of them, and lighter, soft bars that might get crushed on the top. Cookies not in boxes or tins should be individually wrapped in plastic.

Seal the box according to the carrier's requirements. Mark as fragile, and designate clearly on the box which side is up. In general, it is preferable to ship food by Second Day Air, in order to preserve maximum freshness. Now sit back, relax, and eat the cookies you have saved for yourself.

CHOCOLATE ALMOND SHORTBREAD, PAGE 50

16

CINNAMON STARS, PAGE 14

The
Recipes

*Sugar Cookies*

Whatever the holiday, you will be able to find cookie cutters to match. These sugar cookies can be shaped as Christmas trees, jack-o'-lanterns, turkeys, shamrocks, hearts, flags, and a variety of other symbols, and then decorated with frosting in appropriate colors. Easter eggs with pastel stripes look pretty, and heart shapes frosted red make attractive Valentines.

| | |
|---|---|
| ½ cup butter | 1½ cups flour |
| ¾ cup sugar | ¼ teaspoon salt |
| 1 egg | ¼ teaspoon baking powder |
| ½ teaspoon vanilla | 1 tablespoon milk |

Cream together butter and sugar until light and fluffy, then beat egg and vanilla in well. Sift together flour, salt, and baking powder, then mix them into the creamed mixture along with the milk. Wrap dough in waxed paper and chill for about an hour.

Roll out dough on a lightly floured surface until thin. Cut with cookie cutters or a knife into desired shapes, and transfer them to ungreased baking sheets. Bake at 375°F for about 8 minutes, until lightly golden around the edges (the thinner you roll the dough, the less time they will take to cook). Cool a moment on the sheets, then move to wire racks to cool completely.

Once cooled, you may decorate them with royal icing or decorator's frosting (see opposite page), in any way you wish. Makes about 30 cookies.

## Decorator's Frosting

**2 tablespoons butter**
**2 tablespoons milk**
**Confectioner's sugar (up to 1 pound)**
**Food coloring**

Melt butter and add milk. Beat in enough confectioner's sugar to make a stiff frosting that will hold its shape when spread. Tint with a few drops of food coloring. Store in covered containers in the refrigerator.

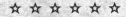

## Royal Icing

**Confectioner's sugar**
**Water**

Mix confectioner's sugar with water. Stir together to form a paste that has a medium consistency.

*Peppermint Candy Canes*

Children will love making and eating candy cane cookies. They are lovely enough to be hung on the tree or used as a bright garnish for gift boxes of cookies.

| | |
|---|---|
| ¾ cup softened butter | 2 cups flour |
| ¾ cup sugar | ½ teaspoon salt |
| 1 egg | ¼ teaspoon baking powder |
| ½ teaspoon vanilla | 1 teaspoon red food coloring |
| ½ teaspoon peppermint extract | |

Cream together butter and sugar, and beat in egg, vanilla, and peppermint extract. Sift flour, salt, and baking powder together, and stir into the creamed mixture. Divide dough in half, and add red food coloring to one of the halves. Wrap each in waxed paper and chill for about 30 minutes.

Divide red half and white half of dough into 30 balls each. Work with groups of 5 balls of each color at a time, keeping the rest chilled. Roll each ball into a 5-inch rope. To form a cookie, pinch the ends of a red and a white rope together, and gently twist. Pinch other ends together, place on an ungreased baking sheet, and curve to make a cane shape. Continue until all cookies are formed. Bake at 375°F for 10 minutes, then transfer to wire racks to cool. Makes 30 canes.

## Christmas Card Cookies

Whether they are used as edible Christmas cards or tags attached to holiday gift packages, these spicy cookies are delicious.

| | |
|---|---|
| 1 teaspoon baking soda | ½ teaspoon salt |
| 1 cup molasses | ⅔ cup margarine |
| 4 cups flour | ¾ cup sugar |
| 1½ teaspoons ginger | ¼ cup orange juice |
| ¼ teaspoon cloves | 1 teaspoon water |
| ½ teaspoon nutmeg | 1 egg yolk |
| ¾ teaspoon cinnamon | Royal icing (see page 19) |

Mix baking soda into molasses and let stand 5 minutes. Mix flour with the spices. Cream margarine with sugar and add juice. Add molasses and flour mixture alternately to the margarine mixture. Wrap in waxed paper and chill several hours.

Roll dough on a floured board to ¼ inch thick and cut with a 3- or 4-inch circle cutter with a scalloped edge. Place carefully on greased baking sheets. If you want, gently pass thread through one edge of each cookie to make a loop. With a fork, beat water and egg yolk well and paint on each cookie. Bake 10 to 12 minutes at 350°F. Cool for 5 minutes before removing the cookies to racks. Makes about 30 cookies.

Using a pastry tube with a fine decorator's point, frost names of recipients with icing in script on the cookies. Be sure the thread hangers are at the tops.

## Stained Glass Windows

Clear candies melted into different shapes give these cookies the look of stained glass. They are elegant decorations for either Christmas or Easter. Instead of using cookie cutters, you can also create original cookie designs by rolling the dough into long ropes and molding them into different shapes.

| | |
|---|---|
| 1⅓ cups butter | 1¼ teaspoons nutmeg |
| 1⅓ cups sugar | 5¼ cups flour |
| ½ cup milk | Clear hard candies, sorted by color and |
| 4 eggs, well beaten | crushed |

Cream together butter and sugar. Beat milk together with eggs and add to butter mixture. Add nutmeg to flour, and then mix gradually into butter mixture. Wrap in waxed paper and chill for 1 hour.

Roll dough to ¼ inch thick and cut out with large cookie cutters of your choice. From the center of each cookie, cut out a circle or other shape using a smaller cookie cutter. Be sure the edges remaining are at least ¼ inch wide. Place on a baking sheet that has been covered with foil. Fill the centers with crushed candy, one color to a hole. If you are using the cookies as ornaments, pass heavy white thread through the top of each cookie to form a loop.

Bake 6 to 9 minutes at 350°F or until candy melts. Cool 5 minutes to solidify candy before moving the cookies carefully to wire racks. Makes about 5 dozen cookies.

23

24

## Pennsylvania Dutch Almond Cookies

Cookies are a central part of the Christmas customs of the Pennsylvania Dutch. This is just one of the many cookies they make for the holidays.

| | |
|---|---|
| 1 cup butter | 2 egg yolks |
| 1 cup confectioner's sugar | 2 tablespoons water |
| 4 egg yolks | Confectioner's sugar (to thicken icing) |
| 3 tablespoons cream | 2 cups finely chopped almonds |
| 3 cups sifted flour | |

Cream the butter and 1 cup of confectioner's sugar, then add the 4 egg yolks and the cream and stir well. Add in sifted flour and mix. Roll out dough on a surface lightly sprinkled with flour and confectioner's sugar, until the dough is about ¼ inch thick. Cut into diamond shapes with a crinkle-edged pastry wheel and place on greased baking sheets. Bake at 350°F for about 15 minutes, then allow them to cool on the sheets.

While the cookies cool, you can prepare the icing. Beat the 2 remaining egg yolks with the water. Add in confectioner's sugar a bit at a time, stirring, until you have a moderately thick paste. Ice the cookies liberally and sprinkle on the almonds thickly. Return to the oven for 3 to 4 minutes to crisp. Makes about 3 dozen cookies.

## Modeled Gingerbread Cookies

From Christmas reindeer to entwined hearts, these cookies can be baked in a variety of holiday shapes. Try your artistic talents in the form of wreaths, Halloween ghosts, stockings, little gingerbread houses, cupids, tall-hatted witches, or goblins.

|                          |                           |
|--------------------------|---------------------------|
| 4 tablespoons sugar      | ½ teaspoon baking soda    |
| ½ cup molasses           | ½ teaspoon salt           |
| 2 tablespoons vegetable oil | 1 teaspoon cinnamon    |
| 2 tablespoons milk       | ½ teaspoon ginger         |
| 2¼ cups flour            |                           |

Mix sugar with liquids and stir well. Reserve ¼ cup of flour and sift together remaining dry ingredients. Add sifted ingredients to liquids, one-fourth at a time, while mixing well. Work the dough with your hands until it is smooth. If it seems too soft for modeling, add a little more of the flour; if it is too crumbly, add a few more drops of milk. The dough should form into a neat ball easily when it is the right consistency.

To model people, begin with 2 balls, a larger one for the body and a smaller one for the head. Then mold dough to form arms and legs, clothing, hats, scarves, and whatever detail you like.

Bake the figures on greased baking sheets at 350°F for about 10 minutes, until lightly firm to the touch. Let them cool a few minutes, then remove them to racks. Store cooled cookies in a tight tin or plastic box so they will stay soft and chewy. If these are to be used only as decorations, push metal hooks into them as they come out of the oven and allow the cookies to dry and become hard. Makes about 15 cookies.

## Gingerbread Cookie Place Cards

To add a special touch to your holiday table, you can use the gingerbread dough to make lovely cookie place cards. Roll out dough to ¼ inch thick and cut rectangles 3 × 4 inches—one for each guest and a few extras to experiment with. Cut an equal number of pieces 2 × 1½ inches. With remaining dough, roll long "snakes" as small as you can without breaking, and twist 2 of these together to form a rope. Place rope around the edges of the larger rectangles to form borders.

Bake all the pieces on a foil-covered cookie sheet for about 10 minutes at 350°F. Allow to cool, then write the name of a guest on the front of each card, using a pastry tube filled with decorator's frosting (see page 19). When this is thoroughly set, attach the smaller rectangles to the backs of the larger rectangles with royal icing (see page 19) to form easels.

*Pecan Snowballs*

You can pile these in cornucopia made of red foil and hang them on the Christmas tree. Or for Easter, tint the confectioner's sugar with paste food coloring to make a pretty pastel coating.

| | |
|---|---|
| 1 cup softened butter | 2 cups flour |
| ¼ cup + 2 tablespoons sugar | 2 cups ground pecans |
| 2 teaspoons vanilla | Confectioner's sugar |
| ¼ teaspoon salt | |

Cream together butter and sugar until light and fluffy. Add vanilla and salt, then stir in flour and pecans until well blended—it will be stiff. Form a ball and wrap in waxed paper. Chill for about an hour.

From the chilled dough, form 1-inch balls and place them on an ungreased baking sheet, leaving an inch between each one. Bake at 375°F for 15 minutes, until cooked but not browned. Remove from oven and let cool on the sheet until only warm, then roll each ball in confectioner's sugar and let cool completely on wire racks. Makes about 50 balls.

## Spanish Wind Wreaths

**F**ew cookies are easier to make, or look more attractive than these dainty white wreaths. They make beautiful Christmas cookies, or piped in the shape of hearts, they are lovely Valentines.

4 egg whites       ¾ cup sugar
¼ teaspoon cream of tartar

*B*eat egg whites with an electric mixer until foamy. Add the cream of tartar and continue beating until they are stiff and form firm peaks. Beat in sugar 1 tablespoon at a time, then continue beating for 3 minutes after the last addition.

*F*ill a star-tipped pastry bag half full with the meringue. Pipe out meringue in the form of small wreathes on a baking sheet covered with baking parchment or aluminum foil. Sprinkle the tops with colored sugar, if you wish.

*P*reheat your oven to 350°F. Place cookies in oven and immediately turn the oven off. Leave cookies in the oven overnight, without opening the door until the next day. Makes about 50 wreaths.

*T*hese are lovely tied with ribbons and hung from tree branches.

29

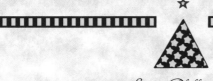

*Spicy Pfeffernuesse*

A Christmas tradition throughout much of Europe, Pfeffernuesse can be made in many different ways. Hang some of these long-lasting cookies in cornucopia on the tree.

| | |
|---|---|
| 1 cup butter | ½ teaspoon white pepper |
| 1 cup buttermilk | 1 teaspoon baking soda mixed with ⅛ |
| 4 cups sugar | cup vinegar |
| 1 tablespoon cinnamon | 1 cup finely chopped walnuts |
| 2 teaspoons cloves | ½ cup finely chopped citron (or minced |
| ½ teaspoon cardamon | candied fruit peel) |
| 2 teaspoons crushed star anise | 3 eggs, beaten |
| 1 teaspoon nutmeg | 7½ cups flour |

Boil together in a saucepan the butter, buttermilk, and sugar until the soft ball stage is reached on a candy thermometer (240°F). Cool slightly, and add the spices. Let it cool completely, and stir in the baking soda and vinegar, nuts, citron, and eggs. Mix in flour to make a stiff dough.

Roll small pieces of dough in your hands, making little balls about ½ inch in diameter, and place them on greased baking sheets, evenly spaced by at least 1 inch. Bake at 350°F until lightly browned. Makes about 350 very small cookies.

## Kerstkransjes

**T**he honey gives these traditional Scandinavian Christmas wreaths a distinctive flavor and allows them to keep well. To hang them on a tree, tie red or green ribbon around them with a bow and a loop.

| | |
|---|---|
| ⅔ cup butter, softened | Grated peel of 1 lemon |
| ½ cup honey | 1 egg, beaten |
| 1 tablespoon water | ½ cup coarsely chopped blanched |
| 2¼ cups whole wheat pastry flour | almonds |
| 1 teaspoon baking powder | Rock or colored sugar |

*M*ix butter, honey, and water in a mixing bowl. In another bowl, stir flour, baking powder, and lemon peel together. Add flour mixture a bit at a time to the butter mixture, stirring between additions. Knead the dough a bit until smooth and soft. Wrap in waxed paper and chill at least 1 hour.

*R*oll out the dough on a floured board to ⅛ inch thick. Cut into 2-inch circles with a cookie cutter or the rim of a glass, and cut a smaller circle out of the center with a thimble, making a wreath shape. Save the centers to make more cookies.

*P*lace the cookies on buttered baking sheets about 1 inch apart. Brush the cookies with beaten egg and sprinkle on nuts and colored sugar. Bake at 375°F for 8 minutes, or until golden brown. Let cookies cool on sheets until no longer soft, then finish cooling on wire racks. Makes about 6 dozen cookies.

## Moravian White Christmas Cookies

These classic Moravian treats are a favorite in Bethlehem, Pennsylvania. You can cut them in different Christmas shapes or just in simple circles. They are so crisp and fragile that they seem to melt in your mouth.

1½ cups butter, softened
3 cups confectioner's sugar
4 eggs, well beaten
4 cups flour, sifted

½ teaspoon salt
½ tablespoon nutmeg
3 tablespoons sherry

Cream the butter and sugar, then add eggs. Sift together flour, salt, and nutmeg twice to lighten. Add sifted ingredients to butter mixture alternately with the sherry, stirring lightly. Wrap dough in waxed paper and refrigerate 6 hours to overnight.

Roll out chilled dough on a floured surface until very thin. Cut into shapes by hand or with cookie cutters. Place on ungreased baking sheets, and bake at 350°F until softly golden around the edges. Makes about 80 cookies.

## Cinnamon Stars

Christmas wouldn't be Christmas in Sweden without these fine-textured cinnamon and almond meringues. If you put these in a box for shipping, wrap each one separately in white tissue paper.

| | |
|---|---|
| 3 egg whites at room temperature | 1 tablespoon cinnamon |
| Dash of salt | 5 to 5½ cups almond meal (or finely |
| 1¼ cups super-fine sugar | ground unblanched almonds) |

Beat egg whites and salt with an electric mixer until they form soft peaks. Slowly add the sugar, and beat for 10 minutes on high speed. Spoon out and set aside ¾ cup of the meringue. Slowly fold in the cinnamon to the remaining meringue and beat the mixture 15 seconds. Gently fold in 4½ cups of the almond meal, until well incorporated. Sprinkle work surface with some of the spare meal, and pat or roll out dough to about ¼ inch, using more meal if needed to prevent sticking. Cut dough with a star-shaped cookie cutter. Place stars on greased and floured cookie sheets.

Spread a portion of the reserved meringue on top of each star, and set the cookies aside in a cool place for 2 hours.

Bake at 300°F until cookies are very lightly browned and tops are firm to a gentle touch—about 20 minutes. Cool a few minutes on the sheets, then transfer to wire racks to cool completely. Makes about 25 stars.

*Lebkuchen*

he ultimate German Christmas cookie, Lebkuchen taste divine, look homey, well, and will keep a long time if sealed in airtight containers.

5 tablespoons margarine
½ cup sugar
½ of a beaten egg
½ cup molasses
½ cup honey
1 ounce citron, finely chopped (or minced candied citrus peel)
3 cups flour
1 teaspoon baking soda

½ teaspoon anise
¼ teaspoon cloves
¼ teaspoon nutmeg
½ teaspoon cinnamon
¼ teaspoon cardamon
6 tablespoons buttermilk
¼ cup walnuts, finely chopped
Royal icing (see page 19)

*C*ream margarine and sugar. Add in ½ of a beaten egg, molasses, honey, and citron. Sift together the flour, baking soda, and spices. Stir flour mixture and buttermilk alternately into molasses mixture. Stir in walnuts, wrap in waxed paper, and chill at least 2 hours.

*R*oll the dough to ¼ inch thick, and cut into rectangles 2 × 3 inches. Place them on a lightly greased baking sheet and bake at 375°F for 10 minutes. Remove from sheets and cool. Paint on royal icing and let dry. Makes 32 cookies.

## German Fruity Spritzes

**R**ed and green jam make these spritz bars glisten like stained glass. Their Christmas colors will brighten any gift box or cookie tray.

| | |
|---|---|
| 1 cup butter, softened | 2⅔ cups flour |
| ½ cup brown sugar, packed | 1 teaspoon baking powder |
| 1 egg | 2 cups raspberry, strawberry, or pineap- |
| 1 teaspoon vanilla | ple jam—tinted red or green |

*C*ream together butter and brown sugar, then add egg and vanilla. Sift flour and baking powder together, and then gradually stir them into the creamed ingredients until smoothly incorporated.

*P*ut half the dough into a cookie press with a 1-inch ribbon plate. Press out 10 strips, each 10 inches long, onto ungreased baking sheets. Now change the plate to a star decorator's tip, and using the rest of the dough, form a rim along the sides of each of the 10 ribbons. The dough rim should be piped on top of the existing dough. Carefully spoon jam down the center of the strips.

*B*ake at 400°F for 8 to 10 minutes. While cookies are still hot, cut strips on the diagonal 1¼ inches wide, then let cool.

## Pecan Speculas

A German specialty, specula molds are a common sight in Nurnberg's Kristkindlmarkt. They come in all sizes, with designs ranging from traditional Christmas motifs to birds and flowers.

| | |
|---|---|
| 3 cups flour | Pinch of salt |
| 1 teaspoon cloves | 1 ¼ cups butter |
| 2 teaspoons cinnamon | 3 tablespoons milk |
| 1 teaspoon ginger | ¼ cup pecan meal (or ground pecans) |
| ½ teaspoon nutmeg | 1 cup firmly packed dark brown sugar |
| Pinch of baking powder | |

Combine first 7 ingredients and then cut in butter until the mixture is fine and crumbly. Mix in milk, pecan meal, and sugar.

Dust the carved side of the specula molds well with flour. Grease cookie sheet lightly. Roll dough ⅜ to ½ inch thick and cut into rectangles the size of the molds. Place each dough rectangle on the baking sheet. Position the mold on top of each and press slowly but firmly enough to leave a clear impression of the design. Dust the mold again with flour before reusing.

Bake speculas 25 minutes in a 350°F oven. Remove from sheets and cool on racks. Makes about 16 speculas.

## German Chocolate Pretzels

Tie loops of narrow red ribbon to these chocolate pretzels and use them to decorate the Christmas tree. But make sure to bake enough for replacements, for they are sure to disappear! For Valentines, you can make them in the shape of 2 entwined hearts.

| | |
|---|---|
| ½ cup softened butter | 2 cups flour |
| ¼ cup sugar | 1 egg, lightly beaten |
| ¼ cup unsweetened cocoa powder | 1 teaspoon vanilla |
| 3 tablespoons hot water | |

Cream together butter and sugar until light and fluffy. Dissolve cocoa in the hot water. Once it cools, beat into butter mixture. Mix in flour, 1 cup at a time, until incorporated, then add egg and vanilla. Form dough into a log about 7 × 2 inches, wrap in waxed paper, and chill for about 30 minutes.

Remove dough from refrigerator and cut into ³⁄₈-inch slices, about 25 pieces. Roll with your hands into ropes about 12 inches long. Twist into pretzel shapes and place on ungreased baking sheets 1 inch apart. Bake at 350°F for 10 minutes, or until firm to the touch. Move to wire racks to cool. Makes about 25 pretzels.

*Brandied Butter Wreaths*

**B**randy gives these Hungarian butter wreaths a delicate apricot flavor. With their green sugar coating, they are an attractive addition to any cookie platter.

| | |
|---|---|
| 1⅓ cups butter, softened | 3¼ cups flour |
| ¾ cup sugar | Royal icing (see page 19) |
| 1 egg yolk | Green decorating sugar |
| ¼ cup apricot brandy | |

*C*ream butter and sugar, then beat in yolk and brandy. Blend in flour little by little, mixing well after each addition. Wrap dough in waxed paper and chill for at least an hour.

*P*inch off small pieces of the chilled dough and roll into 5-inch ropes about ¼ inch in diameter. Twist pairs of these together and join ends to form circles. Bake on greased baking sheets at 350°F for 10 minutes. Cool on racks.

*W*hen cookies are cool, decorate lightly with royal icing and sprinkle with green sugar. Tiny red candies or colored sprinkles can be added to simulate berries. Makes 6 to 7 dozen cookies.

## Caramel Dream Bars

**C**hewy and satisfying, dream bars are sturdy enough to pack for shipping. The oatmeal keeps them moist and tasting fresh. They are a delicious treat for any holiday of the year.

1 cup + 2 tablespoons flour
¼ teaspoon salt
¼ teaspoon baking soda
½ cup packed brown sugar
¾ cup quick rolled oats

½ cup butter
24 caramel candy squares
2 tablespoons heavy cream
½ cup semi-sweet chocolate chips

*I*n a mixing bowl combine 1 cup flour, salt, baking soda, sugar, and oats. Cut in butter until the mixture has fine crumbs. Reserve 1 cup, and press the remaining mixture into the bottom of a greased 8-inch-square baking pan. Bake at 350°F for 10 minutes.

**C**ombine caramels and cream in the top of a double boiler over boiling water and cook until melted. Mix in 2 tablespoons flour, and spread carefully over the cookie base. Sprinkle on chocolate chips, then the remaining crumb mixture. Bake at 350°F for 12 to 15 minutes, until lightly browned. Makes 16 2-inch bars.

## Holiday Linzer Cookies

Traditional in Austria during the Christmas holidays, these cookies are often given to children on St. Nicholas Day in early December. Although they are tender, they will ship well if you make them small enough.

½ cup butter
⅓ cup sugar
1 egg
½ teaspoon vanilla
¼ teaspoon grated lemon rind

1 cup flour
¼ teaspoon salt
Granulated sugar
¼ cup raspberry or apricot jam

Cream together butter and sugar until light and fluffy, then add egg and vanilla. Stir rind, flour, and salt together, then add to the butter mixture. Wrap in waxed paper and chill 2 to 3 hours.

Pinch off a piece of dough and roll into a ball about 1 inch in diameter. Roll in granulated sugar, and place it on a greased and floured cookie sheet. Continue with the remaining dough, placing balls 2 inches apart. Bake for 5 minutes at 375°F.

With the back of a spoon, make an indentation in the top of each ball. Bake 8 more minutes, until the edges are slightly browned. Remove from the oven and spoon a small amount of jam into the indentations. Move to wire racks and let cool. Makes about 15 cookies.

## Orange Oatmeal Bars

Even though they are usually associated with the winter holidays of Hannukah and Christmas, the combination of orange and semi-sweet chocolate flavors in these bars makes them a favorite any time of year.

⅓ cup margarine
⅔ cup brown sugar, packed
1 egg
1 cup sifted flour
¼ teaspoon baking soda
1¼ cups rolled oats

½ cup milk
6 ounces semi-sweet chocolate chips
For syrup topping:
¼ cup sugar
1 tablespoon orange juice
1 tablespoon grated fresh orange rind

Cream margarine and sugar together. Add egg and mix well. Sift flour and baking soda together, and add to margarine. Mix in oats and milk. Stir in chocolate chips and pour into a greased 10-×-5-×-3-inch pan lined with waxed paper. Bake at 375°F for 35 to 40 minutes.

Five minutes before removing bars from the oven, make the syrup. Bring sugar and juice to a boil, stirring constantly. When sugar has dissolved, remove from heat immediately and add rind. Pour hot orange syrup over bars immediately after removing them from the oven. Cool thoroughly and cut into bars. Makes about 25 bars.

*Chocolate Bars*

A favorite Hannukah treat in Poland, these rich, cakelike bars use dry bread-crumbs in place of flour. They do not keep well, so plan to serve them within a day or two of baking. They are delicious served hot for dessert.

| | |
|---|---|
| 6 ounces unsweetened bar chocolate | 6 egg yolks |
| 5 tablespoons margarine | 1½ cups fine dry breadcrumbs |
| 1½ cups sugar | 6 egg whites |
| 1 teaspoon vanilla | |

Melt chocolate in a double boiler over hot, but not boiling water. While it is cooling, cream the margarine and sugar together until well blended. Add vanilla and egg yolks. Mix thoroughly and add the cooled chocolate and breadcrumbs. In a separate bowl, beat egg whites until they form stiff peaks. Fold them gently into the batter, using a smooth, wrapping motion and being careful not to deflate the egg whites.

Bake in a well-greased 11-×-17-inch pan, at 350°F for 35 minutes. Cool for about 10 minutes before cutting with a sharp knife, dipped in hot water just before use. Makes about 30 2-×-3-inch bars.

## Southern Hospitality Lemon Bars

**C**elebrate New Year's Day or Epiphany with these traditional lemon bars borrowed from Southern plantation soirées.

| | |
|---|---|
| 1 cup + 2 tablespoons flour | 1 cup sugar |
| ½ cup softened butter | Finely grated rind of a lemon |
| ¼ cup + 2 tablespoons confectioner's sugar | 3 to 4 tablespoons lemon juice |
| | ½ teaspoon baking powder |
| 2 eggs | |

*M*ix 1 cup flour, butter, and ¼ cup confectioner's sugar into a soft dough, and press evenly into the bottom of a 9-inch-square greased and floured baking pan. Bake in the middle rack of a 350°F oven for 20 minutes.

*A*s that bakes, mix eggs, sugar, lemon rind, lemon juice, and 2 tablespoons flour, adding extra tartness with extra lemon juice to suit your taste. When crust is done, quickly whisk baking powder into the lemon mixture. Remove crust from oven, pour on the lemon topping, and bake for 25 more minutes. Let cool on a wire rack, cut into bars, and dust the top with remaining confectioner's sugar. Makes 25 bars a little less than 2 inches square.

*Orange Roll Cookies*

With their sugary edges, these cookies look elegant on a crystal plate, perfect to pass around at a dessert party on New Year's Eve. They are also durable enough to ship as a holiday gift.

| | |
|---|---|
| 2¾ cups sifted flour | Rind of 1 orange, grated |
| ¼ teaspoon salt | ½ cup finely chopped walnuts |
| ¼ teaspoon baking soda | 2 cups semi-sweet chocolate, finely |
| 1 cup butter | ground |
| ½ cup brown sugar | 1 cup sugar |
| 2 eggs | Orange food coloring |
| 2 tablespoons orange juice | Orange extract |

Sift flour, salt, and baking soda together and set aside. Cream butter and brown sugar, then mix in eggs, one at a time. Add orange juice and rind, sifted ingredients, nuts, and ground chocolate. Roll dough into logs 1½ inches in diameter and approximately 8 inches long, wrap in waxed paper, and chill until firm—about 1 hour.

Place sugar in a jar that has a lid, and add a couple drops each of orange food coloring and orange extract. Put lid tightly on jar and shake well. Pour out sugar on a clean, dry baking sheet, and roll chilled logs in sugar until their outsides are covered completely. Cut logs into ⅛-inch slices and place on an ungreased baking sheet. Bake at 375°F for 12 minutes. Makes about 80 cookies.

## Chocolate Almond Shortbread

**R**eal butter and semi-sweet chocolate make these rich cookies perfect for a Valentine's Day tea. If you want to ship them, cut the squares quite small to avoid breakage.

| | |
|---|---|
| **1 cup butter** | **1½ cups flour** |
| **½ cup packed brown sugar** | **Dash of salt** |
| **½ cup sugar** | **1 cup semi-sweet chocolate** |
| **1 egg yolk** | **¾ cup slivered toasted almonds** |
| **1 teaspoon vanilla** | |

*T*o make base, cream butter and sugars until light and fluffy, then mix in yolk, vanilla, flour, and salt. Pat evenly into the bottom of a small greased jellyroll pan, and bake at 325°F for about 30 minutes, until golden brown. Remove from oven and cool 10 minutes.

*W*hile the base cools, melt the chocolate in the top of a double boiler over simmering water. Spread over the cookie base, and sprinkle on slivered almonds. Let cool until chocolate is set, then cut into squares or diamonds. Makes about 30 bars 1½ × 2 inches.

## Snowflake Spritzes

Spritz presses have a variety of pattern disks, so you can vary them to suit the holiday. Use red dough for Valentine hearts, or pastels with the snowflake disk for flower cookies to fill May baskets. Tint the dough green for trees or shamrocks.

| | |
|---|---|
| 1 cup margarine | 1 teaspoon finely grated orange peel |
| 3 ounces cream cheese | 2½ cups sifted flour |
| 1 cup sugar | ½ teaspoon salt |
| 1 egg yolk | ¼ teaspoon cinnamon |
| 1 teaspoon vanilla | |

Cream margarine and cream cheese well, then gradually cream in the sugar. Beat in egg yolk, vanilla, and orange peel. Sift flour, salt, and cinnamon together, and add to creamed mixture.

Choose pattern disk, and put it in the machine. Put dough into cookie press, packing well to avoid air pockets. Stand press on an ungreased baking sheet, and expel just enough dough for 1 cookie. Do not raise the press from the cookie sheet until enough dough has been forced through to form a cookie. Repeat for each cookie until dough is used up. Bake at 350°F for 12 to 15 minutes, until lightly golden around the edges. Move to wire racks to cool.

If you wish, you can decorate these before baking by sprinkling raw cookies with colored sugar, cinnamon sugar, or chopped nuts. Makes about 70 small cookies.

## Chocolate Cherry Nut Squares

A modern classic, these chewy, goodie-filled bars brighten up any holiday. Use red cherries for Valentine's Day, green for St. Patrick's Day, or both for Christmas.

| | |
|---|---|
| ¾ cup flour | 2 eggs |
| 1 teaspoon baking powder | 1 teaspoon vanilla |
| ¼ teaspoon salt | ¾ cup chocolate chips |
| ¾ cup sugar | ¾ cup candied cherries, halved |
| ¼ cup butter | 1 cup walnuts, coarsely chopped |

Sift together flour, baking powder, salt, and sugar. In a large bowl mix butter, eggs, and vanilla. Stir in flour mixture, then chips, cherries, and nuts.

Spread batter in a greased 9-inch-square baking pan. Bake at 300°F for 50 to 60 minutes, until top is golden. Allow to cool ½ hour on a wire rack. Cut into 1½-inch squares. Makes 36 bars.

*Portuguese Cocoa Cookies*

ight and airy, these meringues originated in the convent kitchens of Portugal, where they are a favorite at Easter.

| | |
|---|---|
| 2 cups sugar | 4 tablespoons heavy cream |
| 6 tablespoons unsweetened cocoa powder | 4 egg whites |
| | 2 cups flour |
| Dash of salt | |

*S*tir sugar, cocoa, and salt together, then mix in the cream. In a separate bowl, beat egg whites with an electric mixer until stiff peaks form. Fold in the cocoa mixture. Then, a little at a time, sift some flour onto the top of the mixture, and fold it in gently. Repeat until all the flour is used. Drop by teaspoonfuls onto a greased baking sheet, and bake at 325°F for 10 minutes. Makes about 40 cookies.

53

## *Chewy Peanut Cookies*

hese chewy cookies are delicious at any season, but for a special treat, try rolling the balls of dough into egg shapes and put the cookies in Easter baskets. Oat flour keeps them moist enough for gift boxes that have a long way to travel.

| | |
|---|---|
| 1 cup butter | 1 teaspoon vanilla |
| 1 cup smooth peanut butter | 2¼ cups oat flour (see note) |
| ½ cup sugar | 2 teaspoons baking soda |
| 1 cup packed brown sugar | ¼ teaspoon salt |
| 2 eggs | 1 cup finely chopped peanuts |

*B*eat together butter, peanut butter, and sugars, then mix in eggs and vanilla. Combine oat flour, baking soda, and salt, and mix into peanut butter mixture well. Stir in nuts. Wrap dough in waxed paper and chill about 1 hour.

*R*oll dough into 1-inch balls and place on ungreased baking sheets. Flatten each with the tines of a fork dipped in sugar to make a criss-cross pattern. Bake at 350°F for 10 minutes, until the edges are golden brown. Cool on sheets. Makes about 50 cookies.

*N*ote: To make oat flour, place 1 cup oatmeal in a blender or food processor. Blend about 1 minute at medium high speed. Continue adding oatmeal a bit at a time until you have the correct amount of flour.

*Greek Easter Cookies*

These traditional cookies from Greece ship well, but don't expect them to last long if you leave them around the house. They are habit-forming!

| | |
|---|---|
| 1 cup softened butter | 2¼ cups sifted flour |
| 2 tablespoons sifted confectioner's sugar | ½ cup lightly toasted ground almonds |
| 1 egg yolk | Approximately 50 whole cloves |
| 1½ teaspoons brandy | Confectioner's sugar |

Cream butter and confectioner's sugar until light and fluffy. Cream in the egg yolk and brandy. Work in the flour and almonds to make a soft dough. If you find the dough sticky at this point, you can chill it, wrapped in waxed paper, for about an hour.

Roll pieces of dough into ovals about 1 × 1½ inches, and place them on ungreased baking sheets 1½ inches apart. Stud each cookie with a clove, and bake at 350°F for 15 minutes, until uniformly pale golden in color, but not brown. Cool cookies on wire racks, then sift spare confectioner's sugar over the tops generously. Makes about 50 cookies.

## Hazelnut Cookies

These traditional Passover cookies use ground nuts in place of flour for a rich, tender texture. Packed with care, they will withstand shipping well.

| | |
|---|---|
| 3 eggs | 2¼ cups ground hazelnuts |
| ½ cup sugar | 1 tablespoon matzo meal |
| 2 tablespoons apricot brandy | 1 cup blanched whole hazelnuts |

Beat eggs until light and fluffy, then add sugar and beat until thick. Add the brandy, ground nuts, and matzo meal and blend well. Roll pieces of dough between your palms to make 1-inch balls and place them on a well-greased baking sheet at least 2 inches apart. Push a whole hazelnut into the center of each cookie.

Bake at 325°F for 15 minutes or until cookies are lightly browned. Remove from baking sheets quickly and cool on racks. Makes about 5 dozen cookies.

## Passover Macaroons

You can use almond meal, available at natural food stores, instead of grinding the blanched almonds yourself. The macaroons will be just as delicious, but they will not be pure white in color.

**Pinch of salt**     **2¼ cups blanched almonds, ground**
**3 egg whites**     **1 tablespoon matzo meal**
**1 cup + 1 tablespoon super-fine sugar**

Add the salt to the egg whites and beat until they form stiff peaks. Gently fold in sugar, almonds, and 2 teaspoons of the matzo meal.

Grease baking sheets and sprinkle them with the remaining matzo meal. Drop by the teaspoonful onto the sheets. Bake at 300°F for 15 minutes. Cool cookies on the sheets until they are firm, then remove to racks. Makes about 5 dozen macaroons.

59

## Pumpkin Goblins

A plateful of these grinning goblin cookies makes a great Halloween treat. You can also make them look like jack-o'-lanterns by adding another raisin for a stem at the top, or substitute currants for the raisins to vary their look.

| | |
|---|---|
| 1 cup margarine | 3½ cups sifted flour |
| 1¼ cups sugar | ½ teaspoon salt |
| 1 egg | ½ teaspoon cinnamon |
| 1 cup mashed cooked pumpkin | ½ teaspoon ginger |
| (fresh or canned) | ¼ teaspoon cloves |
| 1 teaspoon baking soda | ¾ cup raisins |

Cream margarine with the sugar. Add egg and mix well. Add pumpkin and stir until blended. Sift dry ingredients together and add to pumpkin mixture. Drop by the teaspoonful onto greased cookie sheets. Flatten cookies slightly with the back of a teaspoon (dip it in flour if necessary).

Using a raisin for each eye and a line of raisins for a crooked smile, make grinning goblin faces on the cookies. Bake at 400°F for 8 to 10 minutes. These cookies will stay moist and keep very well. Makes about 5 dozen cookies.

## Cranberry Boggers

**B**ake these before Thanksgiving and make enough to add to your Christmas gift boxes. The fruit keeps them moist and adds a bright touch to your holiday packages.

| | |
|---|---|
| 3 cups cranberries | 1 cup sugar |
| 3 cups flour | 1 cup packed brown sugar |
| ¼ teaspoon baking soda | 1 egg |
| 1 teaspoon baking powder | ¼ cup milk |
| ½ teaspoon salt | 2 tablespoons lemon juice |
| ½ cup butter | 1 cup coarsely chopped walnuts |

*S*team the cranberries 5 minutes and chop coarsely. Sift flour, baking soda, baking powder, and salt together. Cream butter and sugars until they are light and fluffy, then beat in egg, milk, and lemon juice. Stir in the flour mixture bit by bit. Add the cranberries and nuts. The cranberries will be soft and will create a marbleized pattern in the dough. Drop by teaspoonfuls onto greased cookie sheets, leaving about 1 inch between for spreading.

*B*ake at 375°F for about 15 minutes, until firm and golden. Transfer to racks to cool. Makes about 90 cookies.

## Old Maine Lace Cookies

These homey spice cookies are a favorite in New England as soon as the snow starts falling. Make plenty for Thanksgiving nibbling and hide some away for Christmas. They'll keep.

¾ cup melted margarine     ½ teaspoon salt
1 cup sugar     1 teaspoon cloves
¼ cup molasses     1 teaspoon cinnamon
1 egg     ½ teaspoon ginger
2 cups flour     Granulated sugar
3 teaspoons baking soda

In mixing bowl, cream together the margarine, sugar, molasses, and egg. Sift together the flour, baking soda, and spices, and stir them into the creamed mixture. Place in refrigerator for ½ hour to cool dough.

Scoop dough up by the teaspoonful, roll into little balls, and roll the balls in granulated sugar. Place them on greased baking sheets 2 inches apart to accommodate spreading. Bake at 350ºF for 12 minutes, or until cookies are flat. Allow to cool for 5 minutes before removing them from the sheets. Makes about 3 dozen cookies.

63

## Polar Bear Claws

**T**ender and buttery, Polar Bear Claws are elegant enough for the fanciest holiday cookie plate. To make a lovely assortment, present them with dark chocolate-covered shortbread.

| | |
|---|---|
| 1 cup butter, softened | 4 ounces ground almonds |
| ¾ cup granulated sugar | ¼ teaspoon cloves |
| 2½ cups flour | Confectioner's sugar |

*C*ream together butter and sugar, then stir in flour, almonds, and cloves. Wrap dough in wax paper and chill at least 1 hour. Butter 6 madeleine pans thoroughly. Press 2 tablespoons of dough into each form.

*B*ake at 350°F for 15 to 20 minutes, until nicely browned. Turn out hot cookies on a board sprinkled with confectioner's sugar, and dust the tops as well. Cool on the board. Makes about 48 cookies.

## Clipper Ship Hermits

Originating with the wives of the clipper-ship captains, thick, chewy hermits can withstand a long voyage. They make a great gift for far-away friends or family.

| | |
|---|---|
| ½ cup butter | ¼ teaspoon mace |
| ½ cup sugar | ¼ teaspoon nutmeg |
| 2 eggs, well beaten | ⅛ teaspoon allspice |
| ½ cup molasses | 3 tablespoons chopped citron (or minced |
| 2 cups flour | candied citrus peel) |
| ½ teaspoon salt | ¼ cup chopped raisins |
| ⅔ teaspoon baking soda | ½ cup currants |
| ⅔ teaspoon cream of tartar | ¼ cup coarsely chopped walnuts |
| 1 teaspoon cinnamon | Glacé cherries |
| ½ teaspoon cloves | |

Cream butter and sugar until light and fluffy, then add eggs and molasses and beat well. Sift flour, salt, baking soda, cream of tartar, and spices together. Combine citron, raisins, and currants, and add ¼ cup of the flour mixture to them to prevent sticking and stir. Mix creamed ingredients, flour mixture, fruits, and walnuts all together, and spread in a greased pan 12 × 8 inches.

Bake at 350°F for about 15 minutes, or until lightly firm to the touch. Cut into squares while warm, and decorate the top of each with half a glacé cherry.

67

## Chocolate Orange Cheer Cookies

You may want to present these rich cookies, dipped in semi-sweet chocolate and nuts, in a heart-shaped box as though they were chocolate candies. You can even make them small enough to place in fluted paper candy cups.

2½ cups sifted flour
2 teaspoons baking powder
¼ teaspoon salt
1 cup margarine
½ cup sugar
¾ cup packed brown sugar
2 eggs, beaten

1½ tablespoons orange liqueur
1½ tablespoons orange peel
1 cup chopped toasted hazelnuts
2 cups semi-sweet chocolate chips
For glaze:
1 cup semi-sweet chocolate chips
½ cup chopped toasted hazelnuts

Sift flour, baking powder, and salt together, and set aside. Cream margarine, sugar, and brown sugar until light and fluffy, then blend in eggs. Add sifted ingredients, liqueur, and peel, mixing thoroughly, then fold in nuts and chocolate chips.

Drop by teaspoonfuls onto ungreased baking sheets and bake at 325°F for about 20 minutes. Transfer to wire racks and cool completely.

While they are cooling, make the glaze. Melt chocolate in the top of a double boiler over simmering water. Remove from heat and dip bottoms of cookies in chocolate glaze. Dip chocolated bottoms in the chopped nuts, and replace on baking sheets. Chill until chocolate is firm. Makes about 48 cookies.

## Zahra's Peanut Feqqas Cookies

**K**itty Morse, author of the elegant Moroccan cookbook, *Come With Me to the Kasbah*, has kindly shared this unusual cookie recipe from her homeland.

| | |
|---|---|
| ¼ pound butter | 1 teaspoon salt |
| 1 cup roasted, unsalted peanuts | ½ cup (4 ounces) cream cheese |
| 1¼ cups pastry flour | 1 egg |

*M*elt 2 tablespoons butter in a small skillet. Sauté the peanuts in butter until golden. Let cool and grind coarsely in a blender or food processor. Set aside. To make pastry dough, combine flour, salt, cream cheese, and 4 tablespoons butter in a large bowl and mix until soft. Refrigerate, covered, for ½ hour.

*T*o make the filling, combine 2 tablespoons butter with the ground peanuts and the egg and mix well. Divide chilled dough in half and roll each half into a 10-inch square. Cut each square in half to form rectangles. Form a rope of peanut filling along one of the long edges of each piece of dough, and roll to enclose filling. Moisten edge to seal. Set each roll carefully on a baking sheet and refrigerate for ½ hour.

*C*ut into slices ¼ inch thick and bake slices on ungreased sheets at 275°F for about 40 minutes, or until golden. The spiral may loosen as they bake, forming a comma-shaped cookie. Makes about 12 dozen tiny cookies, which keep well if stored in an airtight container as soon as they have cooled completely.

## Kitchen Metrics

For cooking and baking convenience, the Metric Commission of
Canada suggests the following for adapting to metric measurement.
The table gives approximate, rather than exact, conversions.

### SPOONS
¼ teaspoon = 1 milliliter
½ teaspoon = 2 milliliters
1 teaspoon = 5 milliliters
1 tablespoon = 15 milliliters
2 tablespoons = 25 milliliters
3 tablespoons = 50 milliliters

### CUPS
¼ cup = 50 milliliters
⅓ cup = 75 milliliters
½ cup = 125 milliliters
⅔ cup = 150 milliliters
¾ cup = 175 milliliters
1 cup = 250 milliliters

### OVEN TEMPERATURES

| | |
|---|---|
| 200°F = 100°C | 350°F = 180°C |
| 225°F = 110°C | 375°F = 190°C |
| 250°F = 120°C | 400°F = 200°C |
| 275°F = 140°C | 425°F = 220°C |
| 300°F = 150°C | 450°F = 230°C |
| 325°F = 160°C | 475°F = 240°C |

## Index

**Christmas**
Brandied Butter Wreaths, 40
Chocolate Cherry Nut
  Squares, 52
Christmas Card Cookies, 21
Cinnamon Stars, *16*, 34
Cranberry Boggers, 61
German Chocolate Pretzels, 39
German Fruity Spritzes, 36, *37*
Gingerbread Cookie Place
  Cards, 27
Holiday Linzer Cookies, 42, *43*
Kerstkransjes, 31
Lebkuchen, 35
Modeled Gingerbread
  Cookies, 26
Moravian White Christmas
  Cookies, 32, *33*
Old Maine Lace Cookies, 62,
  *63*
Orange Oatmeal Bars, 44
Pecan Snowballs, 28
Pecan Speculas, 38
Pennsylvania Dutch Almond
  Cookies, *24*, 25
Peppermint Candy Canes, 20

Spanish Wind Wreaths, 29
Spicy Pfeffernuesse, 30
Stained Glass Windows, 22, *23*
Sugar Cookies, *2*, 18
**Easter**
Chewy Peanut Cookies, *54*, 55
Greek Easter Cookies, 56
Pecan Snowballs, 28
Portuguese Cocoa Cookies, 53
Southern Hospitality Lemon
  Bars, *46*, 47
Stained Glass Windows, 22, *23*
**Halloween**
Modeled Gingerbread
  Cookies, 26
Pumpkin Goblins, 60
Sugar Cookies, *2*, 18
**Hannukah**
Chocolate Bars, 45
Orange Oatmeal Bars, 44
**Miscellaneous**
Caramel Dream Bars, 41
Chocolate Orange Cheer
  Cookies, 68, *69*
Clipper Ship Hermits, 66, *67*
Polar Bear Claws, *64*, 65

Zahra's Peanut Feqqas
  Cookies, *5*, 70
**New Year's Eve**
Orange Roll Cookies, 48, *49*
Southern Hospitality Lemon
  Bars, *46*, 47
**Passover**
Hazelnut Cookies, *8*, 57
Passover Macaroons, 58, *59*
**Thanksgiving**
Cranberry Boggers, 61
Old Maine Lace Cookies, 62,
  *63*
Sugar Cookies, *2*, 18
**Valentine's Day**
Caramel Dream Bars, 41
Chocolate Almond Shortbread,
  *15*, 50
Chocolate Cherry Nut
  Squares, 52
German Chocolate Pretzels, 39
Modeled Gingerbread
  Cookies, 26
Snowflake Spritzes, 51
Spanish Wind Wreaths, 29
Sugar Cookies, *2*, 18